WHISPERS OF SERENITY

PAINTED WITH POETRY

REHAN

Made with ♥ on the Notion Press Platform
www.notionpress.com

Contents

1. Language Of The Soul 1
2. My Needs 2
3. Sharing Is Caring 3
4. Every Inch Of Your Beauty 5
5. I Fell For You 7
6. Ray Of Hope 8
7. Drawn Towards You For A Reason. 9
8. It's About You 11
9. Love Is There To Survive. 13
10. I Want To Shine Like A Star. 15
11. My Sweet Mommy 16
12. You Are The Reason 17
13. Some Stories Are Meant To Be Buried 18
14. Destined For You 20
15. Bang And It Began 21
16. Free Bird 23
17. Never Complain 24
18. I Did All I Can 25
19. Thank You For Not Being There 26
20. My Love For My Daddy 27
21. Perplexed 28
22. Science Defines God 29
23. Never Give Up The Goodness Within You 32
24. Your Overwhelming Presence 34

1. Language of the soul

Poetry is the language of the soul , one of the finest form of art
Driven by echoes of the expressions and enchanted heart
Communicating explicitly different shades of emotions
Sometimes evoking grief , anger, and sometimes impulsive passions
Dancing with words , drowning with veins of verses
Focused on emancipation from depravity , detaching mankind from evil forces
Eruption of thoughts to ponder upon
Forcing us to realize , setting dreams to act on
Giving rise to selflessness and humility
Breaking the chains of arrogance and vanity
Delving into imaginative thoughts drawing reflections of reality
It's a treat for all ages and a tool for empowering mankind
Healing the broken hearts and therapy for fractured minds

2. My needs

I don't want to be rich for the depravity it brings
I don't want to be poor as to scrupulous morality it always clings

I don't want to forsake loneliness for the relief it gives at being not judged
I don't want to be abandoned either for it causes my hope and conscience to plunge.

I don't want to be submissive for slavery it carries and promotes
I don't want to be dominant for the fear it instills and arrogance it supports.

I want to be a human for mistakes he makes.
And to amend them he finds different ways

I want to be loved for the flaws I own
and wish to be nurtured patiently until i have grown.

3. Sharing is caring

My story of sorrow which she tried to borrow
Was deep-filled , with emotions and guilt
To which she brought consolation, pity and stilled
And made me learn lessons on which life is to be re-built
Amazed by her kindness beyond belief
Her words of compassion gave me a soothing relief

When things let you down
as u think there's no one around
And then a moment arise
Erupting as a surprise
Bringing some happiness
To my wretched and gloomy eyes
She shares her pain one fine day
Which paved the way for me to show unconditional concern
And provide comfort to her heart & mind ladened with dismay
I inquired about her health without any delay
Waiting for her reply all of the nights and all of the day
This cycle repeated another day
Wanted to know if she was okay
The reason of my empathy started with an ecstasy
Making me dive to a pool of fantasy.

Unable to figure out if it was due to care or a mere courtesy

4. Every inch of your beauty

Every inch of ur beauty I revered,
Beauty which is not bound by physical dimensions but instead has smell of graciousness.
All the nights and all the days, I admired and glorified
Giving rise to flames of new desire that had nowhere to hide
Which though made me sometimes terrified
As I was carrying along with me a mountain built of deep guilt
Kept on haunting me until it made me sinned.
Nowhere to go but walk down the lanes
Knocking my heart your memory came
Realizing this gave me chills but
Never it did bring me shame
Because Every inch of ur beauty I glorified

Your eyes do tell me that
You have something to say
No matter what come may
You will be always there to stay
This gives me a feeling of joy amidst darkest of times.
In turn I surrender to express my feelings to you in terms of rhymes

Deep down this fact makes me tremble
That I cannot have you
But still there is hope that one day my heart will be replenished by the love
Which I have for you
Glad that I don't see u in my dreams as I know they will never be true
I yearn you to be my reality and wish that death come to me no soon coz I yearn to grow old with you ..

5. I fell for you

I fell for your smile in spite of it being not unique.
I fell for your eyes in spite of it being not divine
I fell for your words despite it being not aligned with thoughts of mine
Candid and bold but it did had fragrance of heavenly cuisine
There is hundred miles between us now
It makes me sometimes ponder how
Our bonding will grow so strong
It makes me crazy all along.
The time we spent apart will make our that bond grow stronger.
But it hurt so bad i can't take it any longer.

6. Ray of Hope

I once heard my mom saying.
From water came this life into being
For verily it quenches all the thirst
But there are some thirsts to ponder upon
Kings with pride have come and gone.
Having thirst of greed and power
Crime against humanity, murders and assaults were their fame.
Neither had any remorse nor shame
Now though kings and their kingships are over
Still nothing has changed in the course
With today's so-called men of valor
Inheriting the same thirst of greed, pride, and power
Light of hope will rekindle the fire of darkness one day
When evil have no place to hide, and virtue will make merry that day.
Will substantiate the fact that we came from water and not only clay

7. Drawn towards you for a reason.

Drawn towards you for a reason
I may be new and amateur in showcasing my love and affection
but my praise carries emotion which is though light like a feather but is deeper like an ocean.
No matter you conceal your valor and supremacy
It will be always poised by your humbleness simplicity.
Not everyone on my list is worthy of being called a hero
Beauty lies in the eye of beholder and doesn't matter even if the world called you a zero
Had always admired you with sole intention of honesty and selflessness.
We all carry that facade to paint the sadness, desolation and unhappiness with joy and cheerfulness
But only few thrives and survives in this journey of sanity , vanity and depravity.
Overburdened with expectations we often tend to break apart and let loose our consciousness eventually ending up like puppets in the hands of self-appointed masters
A human is bound to make mistakes breaking trust, hopes , faith for his own sake
I am no one to complain.

Being born with same features of humane

It's not that I am pretending but maybe I am dreaming
For this dream has plentiful bounties blessing me , you as a guidance and a companion.
The materialistic fancies of the world may be filled with fallacies and illusion
But in you I find a substance and a reality devoid of any delusion

8. It's about you

It all began with her smile
So innocent and agile
Gentle in manners, Polite in her talks
It was so easy to comprehend and grasp her thoughts.,

Though many, not all of my poems had reflections of you
But trust me this poem is for you to you and all about you
My heart sparkle as your glittering eyes twinkle
My body shivers as my eyes behold a glance of your peerless beauty.
My mind goes shallow when you talk so deep and with grace
With speechless voice lost from within , can't help me but find words of praise

For the person you are and for the joy you bring
Makes you as raw and sweet as a shiny apple falling in a spring

Innocence in your eyes cannot be hidden
Charm you possess cannot be unwritten.

How special are you not easy to define
Presence of yours is enough to feel divine

Makes me sometimes lost in the dark nights and arise in the mornings shine

Let this poem be witness and make you always remember
That I finally had the courage to expose my feelings this September

For I know that I am not committing a sin.
For I know that there are obstacles and barriers both outsides and within.

Let this be a one-way traffic of heart pounding through.
Let the feelings be one sided but true.
And let me reiterate.
It was and will always be about you

9. Love is there to survive.

Love was there before it all began
Survived so long , every time grew strong.
thriving all seasons
Blooming in all generations

Love has many shades
Comes in many prices
Seldom lasts eternal
Often tends to fade

Every eye has a story to be heard
Of an embarking journey which we call love
Has spirit to conquer the world like a free bird.

Presence of our soul
Resonates with beating of our heart
Hate and pride evades away with death
Love remains and grows and to many it consoles

Life is full of struggles and battles.
We fight with mind baffled and puzzled
Heart pities us for it knew it has to die
Liberating the soul from life which has nowhere to hide

but love , caressed, flourished and eternally survived

No matter you grow old trying to control
the distressed mind which you call genius , is full of
loopholes .
Love bridges the gap between a barren heart and a fertile
soul.

10. I want to shine like a star.

I want to shine like a star , in the night so bright
Sing like a bird and fly like a kite

Dive in the ocean and swim in the sky
Always make a smiley face and never want to cry

I want to dance with the moon and float with the cloud
get wet in the rain while playing on the ground

I want to be strong and tall ,
like the big trees growing from the plant so small

I feel sad why planets are so far
I cannot even see them from my daddy's car

Thanks to the God for this wonderful life
Thanks to the teachers for being my guide
Thanks to my parents till all the lifetime
Thanks all of you for listening this rhyme.

11. My sweet mommy

My mommy sweet mommy
She loves me so much
She always stands beside me when I needed her touch
My mommy sweet mommy
Bakes me a cake , coated with love cherries and dates
Whenever I'm hungry she cooks me the food
Filling up my plate , she changes my mood.
My mommy sweet mommy
pls don't cry when I am hurt and down
I will fall and learn then stand on my own
I want u to be happy and say this so loud
While u r sleeping and resting, I try to make you proud
My mommy sweet mommy
There's no one like u
You can't live without me
And I can't live without u
My mommy sweet mommy
U have made me a warrior and like a bird who is free
But I am weak and shallow.
If u r not there around me
In this dark and gloomy world always be my shadow
I would break down and lose hope
Mommy sweet mommy, Never leave me and ever go

12. You are the reason

You are cure to my ailing heart , guide to my lost direction
You quench my thirst for tranquility by showing immense affection
You fulfill my desire which were submerged under the rocks of isolation
You made me cross all barriers without the need of other's approbation
Your stood beside when I went through all forms of dejection
You are the reason in establishing in us a divine connection.

13. Some stories are meant to be buried

Call it my choice , inevitable feeling , mental discord
between my heart and mind
or a will from God in me which he designed
Skipped a beat when I first saw you
All of me has fallen for all of you
There's no one around who cures my broken heart more than
you
You are the reason of my happiness which has recently carved
its way out of sadness
Giving light and hope to my life full of persistent darkness
Come what may for I will behold the beauty of our relation
Trust me this will prevail till eternity in all situation
U have the right to treat me a stranger
But never will I ever complain for I know attachment comes
with lot of danger
For me this feeling is though not new
But this one is hitting different and deep
Wish if you only could knew
Its not surprising that one day i will be left broke and
forgotten
distress will though strike me but no qualms since I have
been through these quite often

Will wish you a happy life wherever you go
I may not be with you to remind
that your are one of God's beautiful find
I may not choose to erase the memories we made together
For I know they were bound to remain preserved forever
Your words were like warm sunrise in the cold winter
Melted my frozen soul giving me a new life and a reason to ponder
I want to buy clothes for u , take u for a ride
Watch movies with cup of coffees and eating chickens that are fried
I want to grow old with u , shedding tears together.
holding our weak and fragile hands living alone like strangers
away from all chaos leaving aside all the worldly gains and pleasure
I felt into your eyes which were observant and wide
the rapport between us grew strong with all smiles that u can't hide
With all boxes ticked it made me realize that our future is really bright
Even if the whole world goes against us , the good God is on our side
You may consider me out of your league
Ignore me forsake me.
Leaving my heart to bleed
I will stay strong and stay calm.
For I know some stories of love is meant to be buried

14. Destined for you

I was yours and will always be
Nowhere to go nowhere to hide
If ever u leave me alone in this journey of an amazing ride
I know that I am guilty.
But I can fix it and make you happy
Shattered I will be if you turn your back on me
Sometimes I do lie , it may be not to hurt you
I do lose control and go crazy , but I do all I can do make u smile and please u
Stay with me , things will always be as it was meant to be
We live together but I die before
It's written in the destiny

15. Bang and it began

From a bang so loud , it all began

Creating particles from tiny to large
It was all decided as a part of his plan

Expanded and stretched farthest from our site
He created the Earth and its days and night

Universe came into being , upon his command and order
Originated space time and matter

Doesn't end here the tales of his might
Glorify him as he is the creator of stars which is shining so bright!

Denying his existence is nothing but our plight
apparent and visible are his signs
Expressing us to come from darkness to light
Yet we are so ignorant and
Lost in our ignorance
Little do we notice the signs of his design
Earth its moon and the sun are so perfectly aligned

His anger is limitless and so is his mercy and compassion
Yet we do not care instead feel proud in our transgression

He does not need us, but we do need him
His remembrance gives calmness to our heart and solace to out mind
There's is no one and will never be ever that of his kind

Worship him alone and do his glorification.
Came and gone many tribes and nation
Some believed and some perished
Asking reasons and his proof
Let this be straight that best explanation does not requires an explanation

16. Free bird

Swinging on a swing
So high I am flying
Up and down I am rising and diving
Lost in my own world, all worries and anxieties i have kept on ignoring.

Not afraid of falling , watching birds sing and dance in the sky
Makes me feel jealous and wonder why I am so shy
So much stuff to do once I touch the ground
I feel so jovial and spellbound.

Mommy's not here to lecture and punish
Delighted at this moment , I am here to flourish

It's a bright sunny day ,
Want to be left alone during my journey all the way
Don't want to judged or punished and get distressed
Enjoying every moment on my deserving holiday

17. Never complain

Life will be easy if u fix things than blame
Go through the pain than complain
Be the change than forcing people for the same
Let turmoil not stop you from the fight
Half the battle is won when you are on the path of right.
Let courage overpower the deep rooted fear
Finding the reason to rejoice little did you know that victory is not easy but surely very near

18. I did all I can

I did all I can
Nothing went as per plan

Cursing myself all along
Clueless and crestfallen
Unable to figure out what went wrong.

Hiding myself from me
Never imagined what losing could be

Amidst darkness got some hope of becoming a hero
I can still fix things and rebuild things from zero

Soon the feeling dawned
I was sincere and worked hard
Was silly at times but not fraud

I can rise and fall as ,
I am just a man not God

19. Thank you for not being there

Thank you for clearing the air which was polluted by my love for you
Thank you for demolishing the pillar of trust that had foundation of shallow promises of which I had no clue
I was gentle at times when you were hard at me but thank you for not reciprocating it and having no idea what I went through.
Thank you for making me understand that my feelings are nothing but dust for you ,
Thank you for granting me the freedom which I was longing since I first met you.

20. My love for my Daddy

Oh my Daddy
Do not be angry , you know I strive to make you happy
I will do my best to not make you upset
I will never ever let you down
And will focus on my work even when there's no one around.

But to be very honest
I am not a boy with perfection
If ever I fail a test
Pls don't be upset and get engrossed in stress and tension

And like every human I also make mistake
I am here to conquer hearts and not to be a fake

I may not be the perfect boy
But I'll make sure your cheeks are dry
I'll wipe away all your tears
Throughout the rest of my years

21. Perplexed

So lonely so sad , I am going so mad
Clueless and curios is right now my mind
I have nowhere to go , I nowhere belong
Trying to figure out what had went wrong
Deprived of love and devoid of care
Craving for that moment
Forcing my mind to be strong and agile
Longing for smile , willing to go the extra mile

22. Science defines God

Science should be a tool to define God and not deny God
God wants us to reach him through exploration of science
The glory he owns and the miracles he performs though defy science but manifest his signs

His fingerprint can be found all around
Manifestation of his skill is also profound
and not bound by limited inventions and discoveries scientists has newly found

Evolution of knowledge and wisdom
is more important than evolution of ape kingdom and species mutating random

Purpose of lives is intuitive and empowering.
Elevating our existence from mere product of matter to conscious being
It amuses me how they find it rationally sane to believe we came into being from nothing.
But find it irrational that one responsible for our creation is none other than a powerful being

Existence of world is a physical necessity.

and not mere a chance and contingency

Science explains the cause and effect of a process
fails to dig deep in the foundational and transcendent aspects
.
but its God from where every reason and casualty emerges

Bang comes with destruction is how we understand from
scientific theory of nuclear fission
But the systematic and constructive arrangement of universe
demonstrates Gods will and his reason.
Basis of something to be real and a fact
Cannot be just proven by empirical experiments and
demonstrations.
Also are the criteria which comes into play like truthful
testimonials and philosophical observations

Intrinsically embedded in us are
mental gymnastics and rational faculties
to ponder on purpose of our existence and find the deepest
realities.

Praise be to the Lord for creating all what is apparent and all
what is hidden
Directs us to abide by his laws and forsake what is forbidden

Dark matter , multiverse are some of the theories and

discoveries
Baffle us as we are surrounded by numerous unlocked mysteries.

Mission is not achieved by a false vision
Truth never fades away by falsification.
God is the answer of all our toughest questions

No matter how breathtaking and beautiful the painting is displayed
It's of no worthy if u deny its deserving painter who has got this made .

23. Never give up the goodness within you

A heartfelt note and I will be gone with the wind that would never cross ur path
I fell for you with all my heart , souls and my mind
Lost in your world , you were one of my greatest find.
I know all this might look to you bit bookish , childish and indeed stupid
But it doesn't bother me anymore because I want to break this shackle of burden which I was carrying while being cupid
I did all to impress you manifesting my love through poem , humors and amusing acts
Though all looked naive but were not far from facts
I nodded in agreement to all your words and thoughts.
And never had let my different views to get caught.
Your silence paved the way for my misery.
Nothing can heal the wounds of this eternal injury
Such wounds are irreversible they say
Shattered and crestfallen little did I knew
Realization is the key to restore the lost faith within you
Perseverance and patience will make me grow stronger
Will heal my pain during the course of time erasing the memories I had along her

I will overcome this challenge , from highest of skies and deepest of oceans.
For I know that most battles are lost not because you are less on courage but because
you are less on emotions .

24. Your overwhelming presence

Blown away by your innocence.
Intrigued by your charm
From first day of your presence
You made me settle down with so much of ease and calm
Have great regard to your research and intellect
To me It took though some time to sink in and recollect
Found some connection
From the first day of our session
There's eloquence in your speech , clarity in your thought
With every topic discussed loved the purpose you have got
always to trying to unravel some deep mysteries and find a purpose
With your elegant smile and expressive eyes
U make communication look easy and wise
Neither u like to ignore nor to be felt ignored
With so much to speak on one will never get bored
You have got this unique ability to respond impulsively to doubts and queries
Makes learning easy and devoid of worries.
Your humility is undemanding know no bounds
My accent seems enhancing with desire to explore more.
Love the way u pronounce car as "corrr" and sure as "shore"

I wish to continue to grow and polish my skills.
With your endeavor and support , I may climb one day the highest hills.

www.ingramcontent.com/pod-product-compliance
Lightning Source LLC
LaVergne TN
LVHW021202160826
845679LV00024B/2220

* 9 7 9 8 8 9 4 1 5 3 7 0 4 *